Other books in the Sufism Lecture Series:

Sufism

Sufism and Wisdom

Sufism and Islam

Sufism and Peace

Sufism

and

Knowledge

Molana Salaheddin Ali Nader Shah Angha

"Pir Oveyssi"

The American University of Paris

April 5, 1995

M.T.O. SHAHMAGHSOUDI® PUBLICATIONS

M.T.O. SHAHMAGHSOUDI® PUBLICATIONS

Angha, Salaheddin Ali Nader Shah

Sufism and Knowledge

Library of Congress Catalog Card Number: 95-077986
ISBN: 0-910735-94-8

First edition: 1996
Second edition: 1997

Printed in the U.S.A.

Published and distributed by M.T.O. Shahmaghsoudi
5225 Wisconsin Ave., N.W. Suite #502
Washington, D.C. 20015
U.S.A.

website: http://mto.shahmaghsoudi.org

--*-*

Contents

Introduction
page 1

Sufism and Knowledge
page 7

Endnotes
page 35

Geneaology of
Maktab Tarighat Oveyssi Shahmaghsoudi
(School of Islamic Sufism)®
page 37

--*-*

Wherever the masculine gender is used, it is solely for the purpose of linguistic convenience. Since the intent of religion is for the spiritual elevation of each individual, we believe that religion addresses the soul, and the soul is not subject to gender classification.

Introduction

A few years ago Hazrat Pir began one of his lectures by
asking the audience these questions, "If there were
only one in the world, and that one were you, what would be
your name? Who would you be? Would you hate? Would you
love?" Only an instant lapsed before he calmly asked, "If there
were one, and that one had all the knowledge of the universe,
and could respond to all your needs and all your wants, what
would you do?" Then he said, Sufism is about this "ONE".

Hazrat Pir's method of teaching is definitely thought
provoking, and his students say demanding and challenging.
Some say he evokes the same system of learning as Socrates
did with his students. Those who have interviewed him usu-
ally confess that they are totally disarmed by his questions,
becoming engaged in an intense learning experience. True

to his mission, Hazrat Pir never ceases to teach. His main goal is to show people how they may attain the true state of human dignity, peace and tranquility. His definition of the human being rises above social, cultural and psychological definitions.

Sophisticated communication systems have linked people worldwide, breaking down the "absolutes" that societies, communities and countries had defined and kept sacred for themselves. It is the age of relativity. While exposure to diversity has expanded people's vision of the world, it has also brought elements of insecurity and instability into the day-to-day life of many people. When standards collapse and values shift, where can we find the ultimate definition of our "self"?

Hazrat Pir says, "Each person is a complex and unique masterpiece." Most people, if not all, would like this statement to be true. But what prevents us from experiencing it? What must happen for us to even understand the magnitude of this statement? If we don't allow our imagination to quickly define it, package it and file it away, we could start on a powerful journey of self-realization, which would change the entire fabric of societies, human interactions and legal and social systems. This means moving through the multidimensional patterns of social conditionings that have structured our lives, formed our identities, personalities, self-worth, our perceptions of others and our value systems.

How can we put these aside? And if we should put them aside what would be the yardstick with which we could measure our achievements, our knowledge and our understanding of anything?

Hazrat Pir says, "You are the measure for everything." He is often heard saying, "You have everything that you need. All you need to do is to lift the boundaries you have created, then 'reality' will unveil." But if one wants to be this "unique masterpiece", how, realistically, does one "lift the boundaries?"

"Know thyself," wrote the philosopher Plato about integrity; because "an unexamined life is not worth living." From the time of the Greeks, Western philosophy has advocated self-knowledge — internal learning. Internal learning is at the heart of Islam. As the Holy Prophet Muhammad has said, "Whoever knows the true self knows God."

To begin at the beginning — know thyself. The "i", the individual, is a cherished concept, the acknowledged foundation upon which democracy is built. By transforming the "i", one can go a long way towards transforming the greater world in which the "i" lives. The belief in the perfectibility of the Self has strengthened the fiber of Western society and the collapse of this belief in the twentieth century has brought about alienation and uncertainty in modern societies. Untouched by today's social, economic and political shifts, Hazrat Pir represents a strong and clear voice, reminding us of the urgency to know the true and stable "I". In so doing, he reaffirms the human being's capacity to master the self.

One of the significant contributions of Hazrat Pir to the reservoir of world knowledge is the idea that, because the world has projected its divisions and boundaries onto the vulnerable "i", one must create a process for achieving mastery of mind. This is done by first removing these divisions and boundaries onto the "i" through an inner experience of religion that begins with spiritual integration and ends with a complete metamorphosis. It is no coincidence that two of the healthiest and strongest mystical minds of the Catholic tradition — St. John of the Cross and St. Teresa of Avila — learned much about their mystical journey from Islam as it was received into the Spanish Moorish tradition.

Much can be learned from the way Hazrat Pir teaches. Ideally, a student should think: "I will commit myself not to the idea but the process of mastering my own mind and if enough of us do the same 'the world' will simultaneously change because 'the world' is us." A simple way of stating a complicated process, but it is a beginning.

This series of essays, scripts of lectures given by Hazrat Pir discusses his teaching as it relates to the history of Sufism, peace, wisdom, knowledge, healing, meditation, love, prayer, balance, and alchemy. The author, Hazrat Pir Molana Salaheddin Ali Nader Shah Angha, is the forty-second master of Maktab Tarighat Oveyssi Shahmaghsoudi *(School of Islamic Sufism)*, a school that traces its lineage back to the very advent of Islam in the seventh century A.D. While Hazrat Pir's lectures are faithful to the tradition which produced him and which he now guides, they also reflect the mark he has made on that tradition. Raised and trained in the esoteric tradition of Sufism and educated in the West, Hazrat Pir is exceptionally sensitive to the modern world. Accomplished in the disciplines of religion, science, philosophy and poetry, and trained by his father, Molana Hazrat Shah Maghsoud Sadegh Angha (Professor Angha), himself a great master of Sufism and an advanced physicist, Hazrat Pir has, from a very young age developed not only a perceptive and accomplished mind, but also an expansive spirit.

Our desire to transform the world, he teaches, must begin with a transformation of "i" into "I", the true Self. To the Sufi, this necessitates a dialogue between heart and mind. What Westerners call internal learning, or self-knowledge is, to the Sufi, more like a glorified "i" short of a transformation into Self. For example, Hazrat Pir teaches that drug addiction, the scourge of modern society, will elude well-meaning people's attempts to eradicate it, until they understand how to heal the mind of its addiction, and discover the stable "I". To heal the mind of its addiction, one must acknowledge that God, and not the ego is at the center of the "I". Only then is one capable of living a healthy and balanced life.

A serious scrutiny of Hazrat Pir's example would serve the purpose of welcoming a science of mind that may well complement the existing one in the West. Islam is much in the news these days and concerned people want to know more about a culture that is at once alien and familiar — as familiar as the lines from the *Holy Qur'an*, "I am closer to you than your jugular vein." Most Westerners would not have ever read these words unless they were familiar with a poem of the same name by French writer James Sacré. Yet there is a certain basic sanity about those words rooted in a deeper source than that of the creative ego. Heirs of the Greek tradition, the West is only beginning to realize why the heart of Islam seems so close — it has always been there, part of its world, part of its culture, part of its "I" from the beginning.

So it seems fitting that on American soil, a nation founded on the spirit of exploration and discovery, Hazrat Pir has designed and built a memorial in memory of his teacher and father, Professor Angha. In three dimensions, near Novato, California stands a wonderful metaphor for 1400 years of spiritual labor and the integration of the human being's consciousness. There in architecture and here in words on the page, Hazrat Pir encourages the seeker to submit to his or her own metamorphosis and flower like the art of the memorial through the integration of Self, through integrity to the final union with God.

Sufism
and
Knowledge

In the Name of God
Most Gracious, Most Merciful

God Most Gracious!
It is He Who has taught the Qur'an.
He has created man:
He has taught him speech.
The sun and the moon follow courses computed;
And the herbs and the trees
Both bow in adoration.
And the Firmament has He
Raised high, and He has set up the Balance,
In order that ye may not transgress balance.
So establish weight with justice
And fall not short in the balance.

(Holy Qur'an, 55:1-9)

*P*raise is for God, the All-Knowing, the All-Wise, who bestowed the cloak of knowledge upon His chosen, and conferred the robe of glory and balance in its perfection upon all creation; and set in motion the earth and heavens with His exalted grace and wisdom so that they may be the abode of cognition and affection; and within the infinite core of man, He placed the measure of balance, justice and love to be the guiding light for the elevation of man's being toward the Supreme Essence of Existence.

Thank you for inviting me to speak at your university — the city of knowledge and the city of creation, which is the foundation of the universe.

When we observe the universe, we see how peaceful it is, how tranquil it is. The reason is knowledge, the reason is stability. The universe is all knowledge. If it is possible to have stability and tranquility in the vast universe which expands from nowhere to nowhere, with no beginning and no end, then we should see the same tranquility and stability in the smaller units — from the atom to human societies — since they are part of the universe.

Can we agree that where knowledge and wisdom exist, ignorance, abuse and hatred cannot exist? It is in this context that I would like to speak about Sufism.

Sufism is the reality of religion. In essence, it is a method, a way, a discipline that teaches each person the science of exploring his or her being, unearthing his or her hidden talents and potentials, and discovering the reality of his or her being in this unbounded and infinite tapestry called existence. This process is not the result of the functioning of the mental faculties, i.e., induction, deduction, analysis, etc. It is the method and way through which the Prophets attained the state of absolute cognition.

In the teachings of Sufism, the human being is considered as the perfect image of the universe — the macrocosm and the microcosm — from the physical, magnetic, and metaphysical, to the very depths of the black hole, that is, if we can use this image of existence.

Whatever exists in this universe also exists in the human being. Amir al-Mo'menin Ali (peace be upon him) said over 1,400 years ago:

Do you ponder that you are a microcosm?
Contained within you is the macrocosm,
And you are the Clear Book whose words
manifest the inner.

If we look objectively and closely at the human being, we cannot but be amazed and in awe of this exquisite and unique masterpiece of creation, operated by the will of knowledge whose silent hand has unwrapped the potential of beings into manifestations, so that the pages of existence may be adorned with the beauty of its wisdom.

The physiological or mechanical dimension of the human being not only undergoes the total evolutionary process during its life cycle as a fetus — from the mineral form of its elements, to its plant-like blossoming growth, to the animal form of recapitulated development, to its final human form — but also contains all the elements present in the realm of nature. This is the level of the human being that interacts with nature, is nurtured by nature, and ultimately returns to nature.

If we look at the various medical and scientific fields, it is easy to see how complex the human being is. How many branches of science exist because they want to understand how the human system functions? How many disciplines exist that examine and study the mental and emotional aspects of the human being? How many "religions" or "sects" claim to know how to redeem the human soul? Have any of these disciplines come to a conclusive and satisfying result or understanding of the human being?

Most, if not all of the scientific disciplines exist because they want to make the "natural" life of people more comfortable, less painful, and ultimately longer. Have the advances in the scientific fields, or psycho-social disciplines resulted in creating peaceful individuals, societies and nations? Have any of the religious, political, or social leaders managed to do so?

The evolutionary stages of life on earth, and the capacity of life forms to adapt in order to survive, are self-evident signs that knowledge has no boundaries to limit it. Where can you look in this universe that you will not see the manifestation of knowledge?

Why don't peace, tranquility, and knowledge prevail in human societies? Do you think if wisdom and knowledge prevailed in human societies, there would be hatred, wars, and unrest?

The signs and symptoms of disease, disorder and disaster are manifest in all aspects of human life — from the individual, to the family, the community, the national and international infrastructures. The globe is characterized by a pervasive fear and mistrust, as well as by greed expressed in continual struggles for acquisition of possessions and power. We live in a time of immense change, turbulence, violence and chaos.

On the individual level, people feel unloved, inadequate, lonely, and alienated. Fear, depression and anxiety are everyday experiences. Stress levels are high as people react to external pressures. The American Medical Association states that more than 80% of visits to physician's offices are for stress-related illnesses.[1] Alcohol and drug abuse is rampant, as people try to escape the pain and pressures of everyday life. Relationships have deteriorated, families have split apart. Men and women neglect their children. Single women with children have become a new poverty class. Women and children are abused and molested.[2] And suicide is on the increase.

On the local level, the numbers of violent crimes have risen to alarming rates. In the U.S. "Between 1983 and 1993, the murder rate in young men 18 to 24 doubled. In boys 14 to 17, it more than doubled."[3]

On the global level we see the devastation of human lives through increased tensions, wars, and conflicts. In the wars since 1945, 60% of the casualties have been civilians — primarily women and children.[4] Around the world, the natural environment is being destroyed. The air and waters are increasingly polluted, crops and animals adulterated with poisonous chemicals, and oxygen-giving trees cut down.

As national budgets are depleted to fight crimes, drugs, build prisons, increase the police force, develop sophisticated arms, and so on, people are put under further pressure to work harder and pay more taxes. It seems that there is no end to this vicious cycle.

These are all symptoms of an underlying illness that has not been diagnosed. With so much advancement in the sciences and psycho-social disciplines, not only do we not see improvements in human behavior patterns, we see their deterioration. At least twenty years ago there was no need to have armed guards patrolling hallways in public schools, and children did not kill children.

Since the human being is the cause behind this unrest, the subject of study in the various scientific, social, and psychological fields, as well as the experimenter and the executioner of all the laws in human societies, it is important to see him from a different perspective than is commonly done.

Hazrat Shah Maghsoud Sadegh Angha has said, "Man is a complete being, consisting of the earth and the heavens, the first endowed with fierce, beastly, and satanic attributes, and the second with divine attributes, that is, knowledge, cognition, and wisdom; and man encompasses the totality of all objects and thus he is called the chosen of creation."[5]

In the natural dimension consisting of sensual powers and instincts, the human being is a mass of cells, moving and reacting through the stimulation of insatiable needs, wishes and desires, and false appetites. As he endeavors to satisfy these needs and desires to their optimum, he creates an imbalance in himself and in his surroundings. He strives for power, money, prestige, etc. The more he has, the more he wants, since natural appetite is insatiable. All these drives, often spurred by environmental factors, make him like a beast ruled by fierceness and savagery.

On this level of natural existence, like other living organisms, he follows the natural laws of absorption, assimilation, accumulation and repulsion. But because he rejects true balance, he does not control his appetites and desires, and contrary to most other creatures, he does not refrain from destroying and abusing natural resources, as well as personal and social relationships.

In this dimension of thought and tendencies, the human being is a slave to his desires, with no alternative but to follow his destructive master, each desire leading to other insatiable desires whose ends are unknown. Is this the human being who is supposed to be the chosen of creation — created in the image of God?

An important principle in Sufism is that although the human being is manifested in the natural world, his true identity is other than the sum of his natural appetites and behaviors.

Just like other organisms in nature, the physical dimension of the human consists mostly of water, and the remainder is minerals, chemical, salts, etc. This isn't a being. A piece of wood, rock, a flower, an animal and the human are all similar in the composition of the various elements in their physiology. However, it is his "being" which distinguishes the human from other life forms on earth. It is the "being" that has created the human.

It is the "being" who is the subject of the message of the Prophets. The Prophets are not addressing the elements that make up the various organs including the brain, the memory and the senses. They are not addressing the behaviors learned through the various socialization processes. They are addressing the "being" who has existed ever since the baby was born, and continued to be constant throughout the changes that the child underwent until it reached adulthood. Everything changed — the body, ideas, ideals, thoughts, goals, etc. — but the "being" called "I" always remained constant.

In essence, this is what the message of all Prophets has been through time: Know yourself. Know the "being" who is everlasting and not restricted to the body, to desires, and all the action and reaction that takes place continuously. Know the "being" who is your true identity, the source of your becoming, the source of knowledge, so you may live in peace and balance, so you may know your eternity.

Having discovered and cognized their true identity, the Prophets (peace be upon them) announced to the people of their time how they had arrived at such a result. They did not say follow us blindly. They said, put to the test of personal experience what we say. Be like the scientist who endeavors to know to the fullest the subject of his experiment and study.

For example, the Buddha, after having seen suffering, left his life as a prince and embarked on the path of discovering the cause of suffering and how one could be released from it. He did not stop until he had discovered the answer.

Abraham's discovery was that one must shatter all idols, so one can know and submit to the one God. It is through this cognition and submission that one can be released of all attachments and desires.

Moses said, by obeying the ten commandments, earthly appetites and impulses are controlled, and one can live in peace and tranquility, which will result in residing with peace and tranquility in the Promised Land.

Jesus said, you must be released of all your acquired earthly traits before you can enter the kingdom of heaven. He called to him a child and said, unless you become like this child, you will never enter the kingdom of heaven.

And, Mohammad gave directives as to how one can cognize one's true self. He said, "Whoever cognizes his true self has cognized God." To attain this state one must be submitted to God. It is through submission that one's actions will be founded upon knowledge and wisdom, and not on ignorance, superstition, and blind faith. He has said, "The best amongst you is he whose actions manifest his wisdom."

Every single duty in Islam, as ordained by God, is a step and a method toward self-knowledge. Each and every duty has a reality behind it which must be experienced within each person. In Islam, any act of devotion which is void of its reality is considered as null. Anything that comes between the believer and God is duality.

God commanded the Prophet of Islam,

> O Ahmad, if my servant keeps his prayers as those of the world and heaven, and keeps his fast as those of the earth and heaven, and if he abstains from nourishment as the angels, and if he be naked of garment, and if he sees in his heart love for the world, hypocrisy or pride, I shall turn his heart until he withdraws, and I shall not give him the sweet taste of my affection.[6]

If one looks at the life of the Prophets, one cannot but see a stable security, self-control, humanity, compassion, and determination that could not be shaken by the most formidable events. The law that has governed the lives of the Prophets has been the law of submission, and their wisdom and knowledge is rooted in this law.

Unfortunately, the majority of people think that to be submitted means you are subservient to someone. No, that is blind faith, and not worthy of the dignity of the human being as ordained by God. Submission is the vitality of Islam, because of the dynamic evolution and revolution that takes place from the core of the believer, where all boundaries of separation and duality cease to exist, and in truthfulness the believer attests to the oneness of God, by saying, *"la-ilaha-illa'llah"* — there is no other but God. Attestation is not only verbal, but the believer's body, mind, and heart — his entire being —must resonate with the presence of the one God.

God Almighty has said:

> My servant endlessly seeks closeness to Me through sacrifice so that I may love him; so when I love him, I shall be the eyes with which he sees, and the ears with which he hears, the tongue with which he speaks, the hands with which he holds, the steps with which he endeavors; thus he shall see by Me, and he shall hear by Me, and he shall speak by Me, and he shall hold by Me.[7]

This is the law of submission, where the self bounded to earthly attachments ceases to be, and only God exists. The message and instructions of Islam are meant to bring about this revolution in the person who wants to know who he or she really is. The School of the Prophets is the School of Self-Knowledge.

If we look at the human body we see harmony and balance. In the human body each organ functions independently, and yet works in harmony with the rest of the system, for one purpose, the good of the whole which ensures the survival of the part. This law governs all entities in the universe. We see that the fingers are submitted to the hand, the hand to the brain, and so on. They work as one unit. From the molecules, to the cells, to the organs, they work as a community and in harmony with each other, even though they live the cellular law which governs each individually. The reason for this vast cooperation is that each entity (from the small to the large) is submitted to its own inherent knowledge. Knowledge and entity are one and the same.

For any system to be formed, first there must be attraction among the composing elements. *It is the attractive field which is transformed into either energy or matter.* For example, although Albert Einstein discovered his famous equation $E=mc^2$, he did not conclude that matter is energy or vice versa.[8] He only spoke about the two being equivalent (i.e. of equal value). Ever since Einstein's discovery, scientists have endeavored to find the ultimate nature of matter, but as of yet they have not been successful. The conversion of matter to energy and energy to matter is always through attraction. In the fusion of two hydrogen atoms, for example, energy is emitted and the total mass is reduced. From the foregoing explanation, we can conclude that the attractive field converts to the released energy.

For the formation to actually take place, the attracting elements must converge into a state of harmony. For that system to function at its optimum, all elements composing that system must be in harmony. In the definition of a single cell, it has been said that when the physical, chemical, gravitational and universal forces act in harmony, the cell appears (or is formed). This cell contains all the physical aspects of the universe and also contains all the forces, or power, or energy which has enabled it to act and react in its current state. I have called this "The Principle of Harmony".

It is mathematically shown that the energy distribution of the proton in space determines how much energy should be invested by the electron. In other words, the electron follows the field of the proton to determine the energy distribution of the hydrogen atom. The part with the smaller total energy submits to the part with bigger total energy. This is "The Principle of Submission."

Finally, the electron invests as much energy as it is allowed to. The result of matching these two positive and negative fields is light. The energy distribution of the shared light is twice as much as that which each particle would have in space. Half of this shared light leaves this "united" system of the "H" atom. I have called this, "The Principle of Unity". That is, the result of harmony and submission of a system to another is "Unity".

Thus, the "attractive" force between the electron and proton results in their "unity", that is, the birth of the "H" atom. The off product of the "attraction" is "light". As my father, Hazrat Shah Maghsoud Sadegh Angha has said, "Attraction is light and light is attraction." To explain this point, he has said, "Gravitation is actually nothing but attraction between the trapped light of the atoms, i.e., the shared radiation between the electrons and protons."[9] And we read in the *Holy Qur'an (24:35)*:

> God is the Light of the heavens and the earth.
> The parable of His Light is as if there were a
> Niche And within it a Lamp: the Lamp enclosed
> in Glass: The glass as it were a brilliant star:
> Lit from a blessed Tree, an Olive, neither of the
> East Nor of the West, whose oil is well-nigh lumi-
> nous, Though fire scarce touched it: Light upon
> Light."

From the foregoing examples, we can see that for anything to come together there must first be attraction. Then, harmony, submission and unity are possible. The result is light. This is the key to the teachings of Islam, where the power of attraction creates an internal revolution in the believer, until his entire being is submitted to God, and ultimately he is annihilated in the Absolute, and none remains, but God — the light of the heavens and earth.

There is only one law in the universe, and that is the law of "Oneness". Knowledge, balance, and harmony are inherent in this law; that is why we see harmony and peace in the universe. Humanity has tried to establish and implement laws, and to devise ideologies and systems — from democratic to communist — that would make people behave with the same order and balance that we see manifest in the universe. But unfortunately humanity has not yet been successful. Peace and tranquility do not prevail in human societies — from the smallest unit, the family, to the global level.

Peace and tranquility can never be realized unless each human being is educated to discover the laws governing his or her being. By education I do not mean "acquired knowledge", but "innate endowed knowledge." We do see educated people who are abusive, who fight and kill. World leaders plan wars and order mass executions. Scientists knowingly and intentionally design weapons of destruction, and so on.

Knowledge manifest in the universe results in stability and peace. The essence of the message of the Prophets has been to teach people how to arrive at the same peace and stability in their own lives. However, instead of practicing these instructions as indicated by the Prophets, people have made religion a matter of inheritance, ritual, and blind faith, which are totally the opposite of what the Prophets have said.

If you do not have knowledge of something, repetition will be of no value. People repeat what the Prophets have said, thinking that they too have the same knowledge. I may know God, and I may tell you that God is real, and that you can see God, and that you can be in communication with God, but this is my experience. Even if you repeat what I say a million times, the experience remains mine and is not yours.

If you keep repeating the word knowledge, it will not give you the vast experience contained in the word. Similarly, if you repeat the words peace, stability, and tranquility, you will not have gone through the experience, therefore, they will not have any reality for you.

Repetition of any word creates images in the mind which are linked to the cultural, social, environmental, political, economic, etc. factors which have shaped the memory files of each individual. For example, if you say "God" to a person who has been reared in a Muslim country or family or environment, his image of God will differ from that of someone who has been brought up in a Jewish or Christian environment. For the Buddhist, the word "God" will have virtually no image. Whereas, if you say "Existence" it will bring images to the person's mind which are directly linked to his or her social, cultural, etc. environment.

Because all inputs to the brain are a result of the interaction of the senses with the external environment, the information system in the brain, using its data bank stored in the memory files, continuously evaluates incoming information. Based on this process, the brain decides what to do with the incoming information, and then issues its order to the rest of the organs as to what they should do. If the incoming information does not evoke any response in the memory, it is not recognized as valid, unless more detail is provided for the incoming information, thereby making it possible to connect with what already exists. If it is not reinforced, it is not filed in the long term memory, and eventually dissipates. In general, whatever we are not familiar with requires more detail so that connection and recognition may take place.

Therefore, knowledge based on the inputs of the senses is limited and not constant. Because the senses are in a state of change, they cannot provide stability and peace. Knowledge based on personal experience and absolute cognition results in peace and tranquility because it is real, since our "being" is in harmony with reality. Whatever does not match our "being" or reality becomes a source of conflict and causes stress.

What the Prophets have said is based on knowledge. When you repeat what they have said, it is illusion and it has no reality for you, therefore it becomes a source of conflict. Anything based on knowledge is real. Since imagination is not based on knowledge, but illlusion, it does not have a stable foundation and will create stress.

Religion as practiced in most human societies is no more than illusion. People say, I am a Muslim, Christian, or Jew because they have been born into a Muslim, Christian, or Jewish family. Did the Prophets say you can inherit religion? If the parents' schooling, research, life-experiences can be inherited, so can religion. Can you inherit your parents' experience of love? Or, can you inherit what they had seen in their travels? When we speak about it in such tangible words, it sounds absurd. But, if you pay attention, you will see how absurd it is when people say I am Christian, Jewish or Moslem, because they had parents who were Christian, Jewish or Moslem.

Just as any action brings with it its own experience, so does religion. Your thirst will not be satisfied if you imagine that you or your parents drink water. When you drink water, your thirst is quenched, your system is released of stress, and then water has a reality for you. You can apply this to all the facets of life.

Religion must have the same reality. This is why Sufism is the reality of religion. It is based on the reality of your "being", the stable and constant center of your existence. It is not imaginary, it cannot be inherited, it cannot be forced, nor enforced. Having religion must result in stability in your life at all times, just like the Prophets. It is not relative and subject to cultural, environmental, political, etc. interpretations.

Each entity in this universe has its source and center of stability. If you look at the evolutionary stages of growth of the fetus you will see that shortly after conception — approximately after twenty-one days — there is a pulse beat, and the mass of cells begin to form into a heart which becomes the life-link and source for the development of the rest of the organism. It is from the heart that the nerves begin to branch out and then the brain and the rest of the organs are formed. The brain and all organs are dependent on the heart throughout their life-cycle. Even at death, it is the heart that works until the last moments of life, whereas, the brain ceases to work as soon as it is cut off from oxygen.

The point of stability and knowledge is the heart in the human being. This is why in the teachings of the Prophets, the heart is so significant. The heart is referred to as the gateway to the unseen, the heavenly kingdom, the *Ka'be*, and so forth. Unfortunately, people have taken the heart to be only a symbolic reference to something beyond. Whereas, it is the physical heart which is the gateway to the realm of God. Hazrat Shah Maghsoud Sadegh Angha, *Pir Oveyssi* has called this luminous point, **the source of life in the heart**. He has spoken about this extensively in most of his books including, *The Mystery of Humanity*, *The Hidden Angles of Life*, and *Al-Rasa'el* which are available in English and French.

To emphasize this point, I would like to quote a few passages from the *Scriptures* and the *Holy Qur'an* which point to the significance of the heart in the teachings of the Prophets:

> And every wise hearted among you shall come and make all the Lord hath commanded. *(Exodus 35:10)*

"Examine me, O Lord, and prove me; try my reins and my heart." *(Psalm of David 26:2)*

Have they not traveled in the land, so that they should have hearts with which to understand or ears with which to hear? For surely it is not their eyes that are blind, but blind are the hearts which are in their breasts. *(Holy Qur'an 22:46)*

The centrality of the heart in the teachings of the Prophets is important, because it is the source of our being, and it is to our source that the return must be made. From the time of the Upanishads the wise have said: "Know yourself." It is in knowing yourself that you will be freed of your fears, limitations, and the false boundaries you have created between yourself, others and Existence.

The human being is a complete "book". To read this book he must learn its alphabet. The Prophets have said, to read our "book", we must return to our origin, to the source of our being. Hazrat Mir Ghotbeddin Mohammad Angha, *Pir Oveyssi* has said:

> If only the alphabet of the one spiritual book were revealed to man, and the secret of the soul discovered, he would need none of the words sealed in silent books, and yet would know the story whole.

The above is the essence of the message of the Prophets. Read your "book", so you may know yourself, so you may know where you came from, why you are here, and what lies beyond your life on earth. All unknowns bring stress, disquiet and instability in our lives. The Prophets have said that each person is capable of discovering the unknowns, and has the knowledge and the means to do this. The source of life in your heart is the way through which you can make this discovery.

Thus, the true meaning of education is learning the alphabet of the book of one's own being, so we may discover the hidden and unknown dimensions of our being, so our lives may be founded upon knowledge and result in stability and peace.

In my opinion, thinkers and leaders of the world, instead of persisting in designing and implementing an illusory idea known as society, should put aside their past techniques and endeavor to construct a balanced human being and guide him to know his true values. When the true values of one person are totally known, it is possible to design and implement other laws of action that are built upon those values.

In a society where individuals are trained to know their self-worth, that society will enjoy prosperity, happiness and equality, and its members will stand against baseless and unfounded ideas at any cost. They shall know the true meaning of prosperity for the human society, with sound, constructive ideas and action.

The happiness and prosperity that mankind has envisioned and aspired to for human society will prevail only when all individuals — irrespective of personal disposition, but while enjoying physical well-being — will also attain and benefit from an elevated spiritual state. A prosperous human society is attained through the outward and inward harmony of each of its members, and their harmonious existence in a unified system.

We must not think that we need to undertake monumental projects to attain this goal. The solution is to discover the stable truth which is common throughout humanity. The human being in the universal system of God evolved from one source. The differences we see among the individual members of humanity are factors added to the human being's pure essence during the course of his evolutionary development in nature and society. The result is that the essence is sacrificed for its manifestations.

To have stability and peace we must return to our Source, our Origin. The teachings of the Prophets have provided human beings with a blueprint for this return, so the unknowns which are the source of our uncertainties and instability may be resolved.

May God grant you the resolve to endeavor on the path of self-knowledge; may He teach you the alphabet of the book of the soul so you may read the book of your being; may He grant you patience and perseverance to cultivate your being to its fullest so you will be the peacemakers of your societies; may He open the gate of the City of

Knowledge unto your soul, so your actions may be guided by the light of knowledge and wisdom.

Endnotes

1. Stark, F. (1992, Dec.) American Institute of Stress. *American Health*. pp. 42-47.

2. Sapiro, V. (1994) *Women in American Society*. Mountain View, CA: Mayfield.

3. "Gun Ownership Rises Steadily, And Murder Rate for Young Men Doubles", (1995, Jan. 3) *The Washington Post. Health*. p. 12.

4. Haas, Michael. (1992). A Paradigm of Community for the Post-Cold War World. In Tehranian, Katharine & Majid. (1992). *Restructuring for World Peace*. Creskill, NJ: Hampton Press.

5. Angha, Molana al-Moazam Hazrat Shah Maghsoud Sadegh. (1988). *Al-Rasa'el*. Lanham, MD: University Press of America. p. 14.

6. *Al-Rasa'el*. p. 16.

7. *Al-Rasa'el*. p. 21.

8. Barnett, Lincoln. (1961). *The Universe and Dr. Einstein*. New York: William Morrow & Company.

9. Angha, Molana al-Moazam Hazrat Shah Maghsoud Sadegh & Aryainejad, Sirus. (1994). *Professor Sadegh Angha's Theory of Particle Structure and Its Applications (The Epic of Life)*. New York: Vantage Press.

Genealogy of Maktab Tarighat Oveyssi Shahmaghsoudi
(School of Islamic Sufism)®

Prophet Mohammad
Imam Ali
Hazrat Oveys Gharani*
Hazrat Salman Farsi
Hazrat Habib-ibn Salim Ra'i
Hazrat Soltan Ebrahim Adham
Hazrat Abu Ali Shaqiq al-Balkhi
Hazrat Sheikh Abu Torab Nakhshabi
Hazrat Sheikh Abi Amr al-Istakhri
Hazrat Abu Ja'far Hazza
Hazrat Sheikh Kabir Abu Abdollah Mohammad-ibn Khafif Shirazi
Hazrat Sheikh Hossein Akkar
Hazrat Sheikh Morshed Abu-Isshaq Shahriar Kazerouni
Hazrat Khatib Abolfath Abdolkarim
Hazrat Ali-ibn Hassan Basri
Hazrat Serajeddin Abolfath Mahmoud-ibn Mahmoudi Sabouni Beyzavi
Hazrat Sheikh Abu Abdollah Rouzbehan Baghli Shirazi
Hazrat Sheikh Najmeddin Tamat-al Kobra Khivaghi
Hazrat Sheikh Ali Lala Ghaznavi
Hazrat Sheikh Ahmad Zaker Jowzeghani
Hazrat Noureddin Abdolrahman Esfarayeni
Hazrat Sheikh Alaoddowleh Semnani
Hazrat Mahmoud Mazdaghani
Hazrat Amir Seyyed Ali Hamedani
Hazrat Sheikh Ahmad Khatlani
Hazrat Seyyed Mohammad Abdollah Ghatifi al-Hasavi Nourbakhsh
Hazrat Shah Ghassem Feyzbakhsh
Hazrat Hossein Abarghoui Janbakhsh
Hazrat Darvish Malek Ali Joveyni
Hazrat Darvish Ali Sodeyri
Hazrat Darvish Kamaleddin Sodeyri
Hazrat Darvish Mohammad Mozaheb Karandehi (Pir Palandouz)
Hazrat Mir Mohammad Mo'men Sodeyri Sabzevari
Hazrat Mir Mohammad Taghi Shahi Mashhadi
Hazrat Mir Mozaffar Ali
Hazrat Mir Mohammad Ali
Hazrat Seyyed Shamseddin Mohammad
Hazrat Seyyed Abdolvahab Naini
Hazrat Haj Mohammad Hassan Kouzekanani
Hazrat Agha Abdolghader Jahromi
Hazrat Jalaleddin Ali Mir Abolfazl Angha
Hazrat Mir Ghotbeddin Mohammad Angha
Hazrat Molana Shah Maghsoud Sadegh Angha
Hazrat Salaheddin Ali Nader Shah Angha

*The conventional Arabic transliteration is Uways al-Qarani